On the Pond

Written by Caroline Pitcher

Illustrated by Valerie McBride

Rigby

Duck swims out across the pond.
Her home is on the bank beyond.

She swims toward the far-off hill.
Under the water she dips her bill.

She bends her neck
and dunks her head,
and looks around
for crumbs of bread.

Duck swims between
the clumps of reeds.

She eats up all the food she needs.

Duck can quack, but she cannot sing.
She tucks her head
under her wing.

It's getting cold.
No sun at all.
Duck knows the snow
is going to fall.

"Quack, quack,"
says Duck.
"Time for a rest."

When winter comes, rest is best.